# INVENTORY OF A FIELD

*poems by*

## Andrea England

Finishing Line Press
Georgetown, Kentucky

# INVENTORY OF A FIELD

Copyright © 2014 by Andrea England
ISBN 978-1-62229-534-0 First Edition
All rights reserved under International and Pan-American Copyright Conventions. No part of this book may be reproduced in any manner whatsoever without written permission from the publisher, except in the case of brief quotations embodied in critical articles and reviews.

ACKNOWLEDGMENTS

Earlier versions of these poems appeared in the following journals and publications.

*Crab Orchard Review*: "Seduction of a Small Town"
*Poetry Motel*: "Dominance" (Broadside Series)
*Hayden's Ferry Review*: "Dream Spiders"

The author admiringly and alphabetically acknowledges the following for their encouragement, close reading, and inspiration: Mebruke Birgeoglu, Nancy Eimers, Mary England, Jes Gettler, Elizabyth Hiscox, Richard and Krista Katrovas, Gary McDowell, Julie McGinnis, Mary, John, Buffy, and Tootsie, William Olson, Jordan Rice, Gary, Natalie, and Jane Swartz, Tuggles, Pam Uschuk, and (in memory), Catherine, Marshall, and Matthew England, Ruth McGinnis, and Nina.

Editor: Christen Kincaid

Cover Art and Design: Jes Gettler

Author Photo: Gary Swartz

Printed in the USA on acid-free paper.
Order online: www.finishinglinepress.com
also available on amazon.com

Author inquiries and mail orders:
Finishing Line Press
P. O. Box 1626
Georgetown, Kentucky 40324
U. S. A.

# Table of Contents

| | |
|---|---|
| Afterwards | 1 |
| [Global warming is a myth; pesticides not carcinogenic] | 2 |
| [Because in our world, something is always hidden] | 4 |
| [Not out of the woods] | 5 |
| Dominance | 6 |
| [But there's still a lot of good in him] | 7 |
| [From whom all blessings flow] | 9 |
| [Empathy cannot be learned] | 12 |
| Fever | 14 |
| Determining this Extinction | 15 |
| Seduction of a Small Town | 16 |
| [Chastity, justice, mercy, and temperance] | 18 |
| Dream Spiders | 19 |
| Notes | 21 |

*for my family*

**Afterwards**

There was the time we gloved up

    and let the orphaned coons climb our

overalls to nipples and formula,

    and afterwards, rubbed them off,

as there was no mother's tongue to lick

    and prompt; the time we saved Baby Jesus

from his nativity and laid him in

    a crow's nest, while in the hospital

my mother's blood slipped out her

    pores; first one diagnosis, then another.

**[Global warming is a myth; pesticides not carcinogenic]**

I.

At the hospital the whiteboards pose stats

    while the single-breasted walk the halls bound

and concealing ports of entry; rural farming

    grounds, the porous incubators. Robins sift

through the Old English leaves; worms thawed too

    early navigate through crocus; we writhe in

the country like veterans wait for planting time.

    If all goes well, the last week of April.

II.

Tired of poems treading like cryptics,

    the bird speak returns to thrushes;

let's keep to simple song: sugar

    for coffee, a one-item list, a yellow or

blue, some one truth without

    a deadbolt; I'd take a lymph node or

a hand drawn map, else

nostalgia, before this pasture gate.

### [Because in our world, something is always hidden]
*to the Common Fox*

I've seen you just once, but I know better

    than this, this one after dark, back raised and

midsummer-drought-red, State Department Disaster

    Area and Nacho-Cheese Doritos bag (in-

the-mouths-of-starving-coyotes')-red, taller than I

    would've expected, darting past the basketball rim

of the driveway and then gone like in love, gone or in

    remission, out to pasture for a nap, to a den as we call it;

the room in a house for children and board games, and

    later, their indeterminable absence.

## [Not out of the woods]

*How many beds have I*

    *slept in? How many beds have I*

*given away?* The clouds let—

    the rain, it is a cold

fall. The chemo has made you

    lose even your pubic hair.

Even the gossamer

    down of your knuckles.

**Dominance**

Long white hairs dangle

    from a fine-toothed comb.

A single drop of blood

    stills the middle-June evening

as spiders prepare themselves,

    egg sacs centered in free-falling silks.

Cries float the birdhouse:

    we are hungry for blindness.

Impermanence lives this darkness,

    wrens with open trusting beaks.

It's not mother pushing food anymore,

    blue jays pecking through throats

chewed from the inside, widening

    their mouths without sound.

**[But there's still a lot of good in him]**

Start with three boys wound in swaddling

    cloth and shin-guards. Go backwards to

their mother, all sequins and hospitality,

    lap-dancing her way through college.

A marriage is not without its red herring,

    its blows, and bloody mouths. Say

she loved him, but he lost his job. Jockey

    bankruptcy with back taxes, suicides. Say

he took a job driving trucks because, and

    got hooked on meth and girls who vote

towards the right. The fireball of hunting

    season, first arrow, then gun is like an oracle

made from the mouths of all the saints

    in the world. He will try to kill his wife and then

himself. He will shuffle to prison sadly asking

for anything else. In the yard, the birds

of prey understand him, drop-foot from electric

wires, wings clipped in escape. They pinch

the mice from his gloved hand and sturdy

themselves against his departure.

## [From whom all blessings flow]

She is faithful as far as the eye

    can cock. I confess that like most

things seen at great heights I thought

    the great horned was the devil, had

horns. Imagine my rebuke when

    I touched one at the Binder Park Zoo,

its short tufts of feathers erect but

    as yielding as Downey-softened shirts.

I am leaning over the kitchen counter

    when she radios in her landing, and this

time of year, the call is more of a cow's

    dirge, almoost, almoost. Each December

she returns to him, her Marco

    Polo to his Kublai Kahn, but not out

of duty. He will never witness the cities

    of Cattail or Drainage Ditch, Illinois; spoiled

yet trapped in the great red barn of man's

    doing. Hoo-hoo hoooooo hoo-hoo, the glottis

exploding. From winter to spring the duet

    filters the air of everything but song. She

will never guess he is damaged goods, as

alone the farm-hand knows what it's like to lose

a finger to something he praised only

    yesterday. I confess I could not bear the

longing, though I confess that I have

    longed. Anaïs Nin said, *We don't see*

*things as they are, we see them as we*

    *are.* Faith will eat the mouse that is

placed in his talon but when the great

   horned rises into the night with her avowal,

spring rains arrive. Go in peace, go

   in peace, come back, come back, go.

**[Empathy cannot be learned]**
*duck feeding*

Over and across the landscaped hill

   something comes sauntering.

It is Mother's Day and I want—

   *everyone misses their mother.*

Everyone's writing squirrels and ducks,

   so be it! Something comes

sauntering—a swollen and ponderous

   meringue, filled with insects, moss.

It waddles on, a kid running tire

   to tire, as if nowhere else

existed but this present, now—

   *the first star, make a wish!*

In a blink, God-speed, a flick of the wrist,

   the driver races purposely

down the hill or, how can I warn you

    without a violence, without

the strike of my open palm to turn

    your blond head, to sway it from

the abandon that is sure to follow,

    when I tell you not to look.

**Fever**

How guiltless the fan in its blue-gray spin

    the ants as they scale the walnut tree,

acid roots that have breeched our foundation,

    while we watch the red-breasted grosbeak flirt

with the titmice through the single pane—

    There is only one language in this world

and it is not ours, the salooned patrons

    of the future or of this evening's gaze,

the heartbeat of the *Greatest Show on Earth.*

    Dusk resurrects this fever, baits raccoons

with marshmallows. One life for one, trap

    immersed in water, one hand reaching up.

## Determining This Extinction

She still believes she killed her

    mother by stepping on the cracks.

Cronopio dentiatucus, saber tooth, used

    its fangs for piercing insects' plates.

Mothers pump and/or pay, milk like oil,

    mail for variation and prep school IQ's.

*Once you become you cannot leave*

    *yourself entirely.* The breasts gone,

the bones stay, stay from tomboy

    to *Playboy*, and back beyond reply.

## Seduction of a Small Town

Here, no doors can open. Grief and ice

    have swollen into deadbolts.

Three years since cars and plow,

    three years since your body-box.

The wind exhales snow across roads

    like ether. I count the nights

dressed in sweat, naked: close my eyes

    and fall into something uncharted,

white. Sometimes death is a house,

    sometimes a house in winter:

windows frozen shut, only damp wood

    awaiting the match.

Snowbound, I go hunting for things

    meant to be found on days like this—

A light blue wedding garter, a half-finished letter

addressed to me one December. It says,

*School's dismissed early today*

*and there's chili on the stove.*

## [Chastity, justice, mercy, and temperance]
### *Wedge Pack Tragedy*

The last of them is dead. *A wolf is a dog without*

*a master.* Disturb us. Disturb me

when I'm sitting at my favorite steakhouse with

my daughters waiting. Disturb us

by way of hunger. Tell me all the prime-rib

has gone to the wolves. Seduce us

like babies, with something shiny, a picture of

ironic planets, a child with a moon

for a belly, a belly for a moon, a platter of

*I've misspoken, I've misbehaved,* as

perdition decoys its traveler. Forgive us

our habit of eating like wild animals,

charge us for the whole cow, send us home empty

because we kill everything, because why not.

# Dream Spiders

They come in droves and small armies. They come nightly

    in the hinges of doors. Most mornings I am relieved

to find their burnt popcorn-husk backs, the familiar flimsy

    legs of domestics rocking back and forth in the corners of

bathroom windows. I have witnessed the day-moths wrapped

    and suckled. I have seen them drop from the web stiff and

empty. To wait out the death of mothers who outlive their daughters,

    to watch that devouring, when the last fly has been siphoned dry and

turns to the other like a lover in some old Broadway musical,

    with respect and a soft shoe. It is almost romantic, abdomens pressed,

legs leaning in then out. It is almost human that one gets to

    walk, full and lost, waking first, then again from the dream.

# Notes

[  ] surrounding the titles of many of these poems signify phrases that I have heard from doctors, friends, children, and other media sources. Titles needing further recognition are listed below followed by general notes.

[From whom all blessings flow] is titled after a common Protestant and Christian Doxology. Over the years, various denominations have adopted modified versions according to specific belief systems. The line in full is "Praise God, from whom all blessings flow."

[Chastity, justice, mercy and temperance] refers to King Lemuel's discourse in Proverbs. Translated, "Lemuel" means "belonging to God." They are also four of the seven heavenly virtues.

The title [Because in this world something is always hidden] was inspired by conservationist and children's author, Thorton W. Burgess's, *Old Mother West Wind* series.

Afterwards and [Not out of the woods] are dedicated to my dearest friend, wildlife rehabilitator, and two-time breast cancer survivor Mary Rotz.

[Empathy cannot be learned] is dedicated to my daughter Mary England.

[Seduction of a small town] is in memory of my mother Catherine Fallon McGinnis.

"Cronopio dentiatucus" refers to the saber-toothed squirrel recently discovered by researchers in Argentina (2011).

"Wedge Pack Tragedy" refers to the August 2012 slaughter of an entire wolf-pack in Washington State. Since then, the grey wolf has been taken off the endangered species list and is hunted in more that five states. For information on wolf legislation and how you can help, go to: http://www.defenders.org/

"As perdition decoys its traveler" is borrowed from Emily Dickenson's poem, "Risk is the Hair that holds the Tun."

Born and raised in the vast industrial plains of Central Illinois, Andrea England has a growing interest in the effects of ground-water contamination and the loss of wild-life habitat due to the pursuit of economic and scientific progress. She has lived in Illinois, Michigan, Oregon, Arizona, Massachusetts, and Holland. Her degrees include an MFA and MSW from Arizona State University, and a Ph.D. in English and Creative Writing from Western Michigan University.

Her poetry has appeared widely in journals and the anthology, *Gathered: Contemporary Quaker Poets*. Her obsessions have taken shape in a number of different employments including: barista, crisis counselor, hospital social worker, English tutor, editor, world traveler, community volunteer, and creative writing instructor. She has been nominated for a Community Star Award for her participation in Creative Expressions, where she facilitated creative writing workshops as part of the Michigan Prisoner Re-entry Program. She is the recipient of an Academy for American Poet's Prize and a Gwen Frostic Prize in Poetry, among others.

Currently, Andrea England teaches English at Western Michigan University, and is an assistant editor for *Third Coast Magazine*. She is the mother of three daughters, a dog, and five loud-clucking hens.